TRIUMPH HOUSE
Poetry with a Purpose

Absolute Animals

Edited by Steve Twelvetree

First published in Great Britain in 2000 by
TRIUMPH HOUSE
Remus House,
Coltsfoot Drive,
Woodston,
Peterborough, PE2 9JX
Telephone (01733) 898102

HB ISBN 1 86161 770 4
SB ISBN 1 86161 775 5

Foreword

We each hold people, places and situations dear to us. However there is an extra special bond between ourselves and our pets. Our pets stay loyal to us, we depend on them to keep us company, when we feel low, they have the unique way of noticing and making things seem better. So it is no surprise that over 100 new and established poets have united in praise of their pets.

In this beautiful anthology pets are placed on a pedestal and praised for their weird and wacky ways, their ability to entertain, their loving and caring; in fact for all the things we feel are special about our pets.

So sit back and allow each talented poet to introduce you to their 'perfect' pets, time and time again.

Steve Twelvetree
Editor

Contents

The Poems

Twitch, Twitch, Stretch, Twitch . . .

In the middle of the night
From Nowhere
Thoughtcaster Thoughtcaster
Operational
Received by
Atoms and Plants
Atoms and Plants . . . and people

The coolness of the caves
One timeless day
Waiting Waiting
For the IceStalactite
Poised above
To suddenly
Appear to drop
Freezing the stillness

In the middle of the night
From Nowhere
SilentTown SilentTown
Moon without sun
Night without day
Cats Stalking
Cats Stalking . . . Dreamers . . .

Michael Courtney Soper

Boatswain

A privileged friend of Pindar's son
at pleasure returned a hand-thrown wood,
who roamed lush acres honeyed beauty grew
beneath a heaven where broad oaks stood.
He did not know still less could tell
beyond his shore adventures played,
where sun-kissed lands enticed sweet fruits
there quenched loose passions, his master strayed.
A stone-arched doorway in where he lay
his patience swelled as time would burn,
across the waves where perils lurked
his master's haste in time would learn.
Newstead hound who nuzzled a giant
who followed a whistle and heeled a call,
and nestled inside where instinct demurred
to the Devil's affliction his master should fall.
Sore rabid memories for a corsair of lust
whose gentilesse touch was faithful Boatswain,
equals engaged whose souls rest apart
each carried to earth and there shall remain.

Tom Griffiths

Flora - Rebel Labrador

My Father is titled, my Mother well-known
I'm aristocratic as their genes have shown
I'm black and shiny and beautiful too
With blood in my veins all terribly blue

I was born in the Pennines all rugged and wild
Of brothers and sisters I was the tenth child
I travelled to Lincs when I was eight weeks old
The tough man who bred me said I was sold

My new home was nice after living outside
I had duvets and toys and good food supplied
My photo was taken by Shooting Gazette
I was cuddled and loved by the people I met

But as I grew older my nose told me all
I would not listen to whistle or call
One day I escaped to the woods far away
I chased the wild deer and the pheasants all day

My Irish blood made me want to fight
All the rules I knew were really quite right
But now I'm three and have learnt all my lessons
And I do try so hard at training sessions

My 'Mum' loves me and I love her
I've promised my sins will not recur
But oh how my nose does tell me all
I long to race where the birds do fall!

Veronica Michell

To Daisy - Killed By A Speeding Car

Your hazel-amber eyes, once soft with
love were closed last night; their vital spark
extinguished. Yet no bloodstains marred the
dappling of your fur, grown harsh and stark
in death, instead of sleek and warm and smooth
as I remembered it to have been
once, when filled with rapture and with life
you'd lie in shafts of sunlight and preen
yourself, with velvet paws curling and
uncurling in your silent ecstasy.
Oh Daisy, you were loved and will be missed -
For you were never '*just* a cat' to me!

Pauline Mackey

The Dog Show

Last week I went to a dog show
Where a good time was had by all,
But the judge didn't think I was worthy
So a long day was beginning to pall,
When a small boy turned to his mother
And was heard by my missus to say
'Oh Mum, what a beautiful bulldog,'
Which gave us the laugh of the day.
You see I'm an aged Dalmation
And not like a Bulldog at all.
I've elegant spots, whilst he's got a pug nose
And he's squat whereas I am quite tall.

Elizabeth Zettl

To Live Again

I'm Bella's little toy boy
She's come to life again
She was so sad and lonely
In her life of loss and pain.

She's big and I am tiny
I lead her such a game
She chases me and can't make out
Which way I went or came

She hates it when they brush her
Especially near her feet
But I'm so good and let them
I think I look quite neat.

They take us to the seaside
To great wide-open spaces
We have such fun and run and run
I win all the races.

We like to be together
She settles by my side
And then when she's not looking
I scuttle off and hide.

She's always glad to find me
Though now she's not so fast
I think this happy friendship
Will last and last and last.

Josephine Western

Misty

Our photo on the wall of our lovely puppy,
she would run around all grubby!
Loving and funny she was here to stay
mischievous nearly every single day.
When she first arrived she chewed everything to bits,
we all loved her too for her wit.
While she was small she would sit on our knee,
lie under the table while we had tea.
She grew and was full of fun,
always finding the best place to lie in the sun.
As the years went by she settled down,
learnt what she could do and she could not
Full of mischief with lots of affection
Misty was our pet born to perfection
Misty's squashed face and small stumpy tail,
she was so kind and always on our minds.
When she was sick and ready to go,
it was hard to lose beautiful Misty as white as snow.
She is in heaven now asleep and at rest,
we will remember her as one of the best.
So the photo on the wall with Misty and her ball
makes us smile . . . a Boxer dog with style!

Blanche Farley

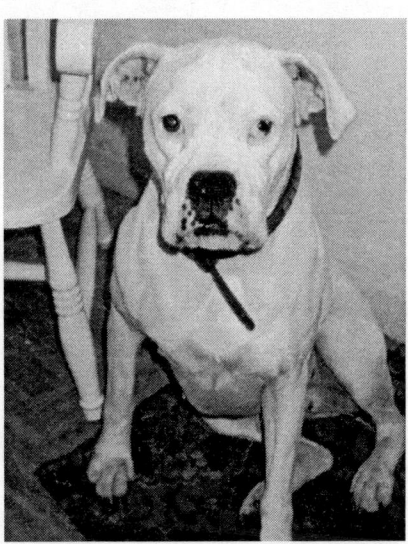

The Black Cat

My mistress loves me dearly
I know 'cos I've heard her tell
She loves to stroke my sleek black fur
And feeds me very well.

I purr when I am happy
I scratch when I'm upset
My basket is pure luxury
The best that I can get.

Fresh milk is in my saucer
I come and go as I please
Occasionally I catch a mouse
But I have a life of ease.

I'm a very obedient fellow
I don't wander out at night.
If the dog next door got hold of me
I'd be in a sorry plight.

I love to climb to the top of the tree
Occasionally I get stuck
But I'm a very brave old cat
I get down with black cat's luck.

I love to lie out in the sun
And roll in the grass so green
But if my fur gets bedraggled
I'm a sorry sight to be seen.

My mistress calls me 'Tiddles'
It refers to when I was young
Now I know how a cat should behave
And I get my praises sung.

Edna Wilcox

Tim

Tucked under his safe arm you came
A little lost, unwanted stray,
Frightened and forlorn - no name
You crept into our home to stay.

A mongrel breed with terrier head
And greyhound legs - we called you Tim,
You loved your new warm doggy bed
And licked our hands, our hearts to win.

Twelve years you stayed our faithful friend,
You were our guardian that's for sure,
We wished your life to never end
But you were called to that other shore.

Now when in country lanes and fair
Amid the autumn leaves and mist
I almost see and feel you there
Almost I turn and call out 'Tim.'

Mary Bowden

Tiki

He was just a dog; a little black dog; with eyes akin to the stars.
He slept like a log,
    did our lovely
      'Tiki-dog'
   'twitching and talking'
      as he dreamt of a 'chase'.
With his whiskers 'Quick-Windmills' . . . his nose wet as dew
      and legs keeping pace with his 'hopes'
    his grunts and squeaks
      telling stories of joy.
On his chest, a white 'medal', we said to show 'he was the best'
    his teeth, so gentle, when he played with his pals.
We knew him so short a while,
     'our joy' - 'our doggy boy'
A 'speed-mad' motorist
    took his life
    'with a bang'
    leaving us saddened, and lonely,
      yet
    with memories strong
    of our love
      for him then;
   and,
      our love for him still.

Gordon Reid Johns

Codge

Each day my newspaper shop
Is prepared very early.
The papers marked and bagged
All ready for delivery.

One winter morning outside
Was a cat, cold and unfed.
Black fur matted and tangled,
'Poor old Codger,' I said.

His life was saved by a vet.
'Malnutrition through neglect
And cat flu,' he sadly said.
'I'll take him and do my best.'

After some time Codge returned.
Fur cashmere-soft, tangle-free,
With eyes shining like amber.
A very fine cat indeed.

Local children loved him, and
Fred, the butcher next door,
Fed him on meat and liver.
Could any cat ask for more?

One day a woman flounced in,
Grabbing Codge who was asleep.
She said 'This is my cat Daisy
Who has two kittens to feed.'

'So Daisy has two kittens?'
I said, and must be a 'she'.
Well, this cat is not yours
He's mine as 'Codge' is a 'he'.

Gill Cordy

The White Stallion

What nobler sight in all Arabia
than the white stallion
wild of eye, with flowing mane
galloping like some ancient galleon
upon the desert sea.

Proud hooves pounding, ears a'prick,
bareback Arab, robes full sail
shimmering into harmony
with the flowing tail
of that majestic ship.

The flaring nostrils, shading red,
determined thrust of chest,
and his the fine-drawn eagle face
that urged it on some quest -
as off across the sands they sped
to vanish in the west.

What dignity, what pride
in this one lonely ride,
what natural aristocracy -
I'd glimpsed the best,
The Shaikhly best
in all Arabia.

Edward Fursdon

Pet Love

To others she is just an irritable yapping canine
But to me; so precious this loving pooch of mine
Are they not aware of the loyalty she dotes upon me?
Do they not know the pleasures that I alone can see?

It matters not to her what moody ways I feel
She shows no resentment when coming to heel
Just raises her head and awaits the next command
A simple gesture appreciated from my hand

What peace I find when she sits upon my knee
This little furry bundle with unknown pedigree
But with stature grand and haughtiness absurd
Never in dispute of my commanding word

She guards me well with warning barking sounds
No intruder dares to invade when she is around
Though small in physique, with stout brave heart
What would I do if ever we should come to part?

But yet with the coming of each new day
I appreciate what I have in work or in play
For when comes the loneliness of evening tide
She will be there; in slumber; at my bedside.

Richard Saunders

Peanuts

Peanuts was my corgi, a gorgeous little puppy
his eyes so bright and shiny, his legs were short and stumpy
His white-shirted coat was russet red
with a beautiful sheen
When I took him for walkies the lads would say
'Oh look here comes the Queen.'
He was always full of energy and loved to fetch a stick
until he put some weight on and became obese and thick.
I took him to Weight-Watching pets
which he didn't like at all when on the scales he
tried to cheat by leaning on the wall!
He got decidedly thinner
His little legs stopped bucking -
He looked so much trimmer
They put him on a diet - he looked so much trimmer.
He was soon back to his normal self and running for a ball
Ever eager and excited when friends came to call.
I lost my little Peanuts just a few short years ago
but I feel his doggy presence still everywhere I go.
Each time I glance about the house I seem to see him there
and walking on our old haunts is more than I can bear.
I know I'll never find a friend so constant and so true
His trusting eyes and faithful love would give me
strength anew.
'Get another dog - you'll get over him' my friends all cry
but I never can replace him - so I won't even try.

Elsie Francis

Triumph House Anthology

The Dog Snatcher

My brother's
Alsation was stolen
outside a cafe in Oxford High Street
on a Sunday the fourth of October.
It is like a death
at first a hope to get him back.
The owner sips coffee
and looks to a French girl.
Doesn't notice a shady dark character
in a leather jacket
entice our beloved dog away.
Jovi makes no struggle to be led astray
grateful to be untied.
You can blame the owners but blame the thief more.
You pin posters and hope for a clue.
Suspicion has it from the proprietor of a shop nearby
that the criminal was of gypsy ties.
We peruse to campsites and caravans at roadsides.
No clues except they trade in dogs.
We arrange four Alsations to view the next eve.
When we meet the date there is only one
too old to be ours.
The gypsies are above the law
possible bandits of the dog trade.
We may have no hope of ever seeing our barker again.
There may be no chance of ever having him home.
We love and miss our dog desperately,
the deceitful dog snatchers have taken him
as a shoplifter would take a fancy
to a dress in the window.

Edward Harlow

Brock And Tina

(Two little Papillons)

Two little Papillons sitting on a chair,
All innocent their wide-eyed stare.
But turn your back
And alas, alack,
They leap across the floor
Scattering biscuits by the score.
Tina's keen to hide her cheese -
Not in your basket, if you please!
Brock just loves the rabbit
And it is his daily habit
To sit beside the cage and bark
And then to scratch around and make his mark.
I can really hear his heartfelt wish
For rabbit stew within his dish!
Then they flash across the lawn,
Treading daisies in the dawn.
Feathers flying in the breeze,
Chasing squirrels from the trees.
Running like the wind
With banners streaming brave behind them -
Quickly gone - two Papillons!

Eileen M Lodge

Charlie

He's beautiful and lovelyful,
And gorgeous and divine,
My World is wrapped around him
And I'm glad that he is mine.

I dare not think of losing him
Because it makes me cry
I'm sure he really loves me
But I often wonder why

I know that he is selfish
That's because he is a cat
He really, really likes his food
And that's what makes him fat.

I know some day he'll have to go
But please, God, not just yet
Because I really love him so
He's more than just a pet.

Dorothy Chambers

Barney

I thought my life was quiet and sweet
Retired at last, my plans complete
To leave my bed when rush hour's gone
Await the mail and ponder on
Of what the day may hold in store
My time my own, could not want more.

Then unprepared was I on sight
Of this sweet pup who gave delight
So warm and cute my heart was lost
He must be mine, who cares of cost?
How could I know what was in store
He ruled the house with tricks galore

The postman most aware of change
Decided he must keep estranged
My knitting, glasses, bras and pants
The toilet rolls and raves and rants
Shrieks of laughter, hours flown by
What did I plan today and why?

Exhausted now I aim to rest
Admit defeat - I'm out of zest
With large brown eyes he stares at me
'What fun we had, you must agree.'
I settle down and to surprise
He snuggles in with half-closed eyes
I'm not quite sure who won this day
But thankful that he came my way.

Margaret Gardner

Triplicat

Vain creature she, who loves to pose,
'Oh, do admire the markings on my nose,
My shell-pink ears and eyes of deepest green,
My silken coat I groom to wondrous sheen.'

But there are other sides to Psyche mine,
An avid hunter, presents in a line
Appeared presented neatly on the mat,
Kindly brought by muddy, 'Beauty Cat'.

This schizophrenic feline's also smart,
She knows the way to really melt my heart.
A conversation by the cupboard door
Will lead, she's sure, to biscuits by the score.

The plaintive voice endorsed by swaying tail,
These clever tactics never, never fail.
But I'm rewarded with a lullaby,
Purred softly to me as in bed we lie,
My cosy, cuddly, sleepy friend and I.

Pat Williams

Lucy And Pickles Say 'Hello.'

Two wagging tails, four pleading eyes
Soft furry coats, that was the prize.
Two little bundles, one in each hand
Captured our hearts, you'll understand.

Two King Charles spaniels are they
Who would hold us in their sway
Bringing with them laughter and fun
Double the trouble, than just one!

They keep each other company
Sharing everything they can see,
Be it newspapers, slippers or their beds
Where they snuggled down to rest their heads.

They will greet us every morning
With a joy that's so heart-warming
Sensing always the mood we're in
With their response all hearts they win.

These sisters - Pickles and Lucy
Are as different as you and me
But they give their love unconditionally
To everyone whom they see.

Joan Earle Broad

Triumph House Anthology

Extra Love

God knew that I needed extra love in my life
Even though I was busy being a mother and wife.
God knew I was lonely as He watched from above,
And so He sent me Sammy to cuddle and love.

My husband and I often went on long walks,
And I'd mention I would love a dog during our talks.
At first, on the idea he wasn't very keen,
But I kept on talking about the dogs we had seen.
I kept on and on, I wouldn't give up.
'Wouldn't it be lovely to have a Cavalier pup?'

God softened his heart and at last, he said, 'Okay.'
And we went for my puppy - I'll never forget that day.
This dear little bundle, only seven weeks old,
So trusting, and around him my arms I did fold.

You'd be forgiven for thinking we'd brought a new baby home
With his basket and blankets, toys, brushes and comb.
Then there's the walking, bathing and brushing,
(Not to mention the housework, with the ironing and washing).
But oh! how I love him, and he loves me too.
If we were ever parted, I don't know what I'd do.

Sammy has broken all the rules - everything we'd said.
He drinks my husband's cup of tea, and sleeps upon the bed.
Sometimes he is so greedy, scratching at the larder door,
No matter how much food he eats, he's always wanting more.
Sammy is very handsome, with long brown curly ears.
He's never very far away, when the biscuit tin he hears.

When I put my arms around him, and tell him all my woes,
He quietly sits there listening, the concern in his eyes really shows.
The love that Sammy gives to me is unconditional and true.
A more loving friend I could not have, and my husband loves him too.

Elaine Cooper

Mopsy

She came to us one Friday
When golden leaves lay on the ground
This beautiful little creature
Which a friend in the garden found.
She moved with the grace of a tiger,
And charmed us all with her affectionate ways
That appealing face upturned and sweet,
Those green eyes with their shining gaze.
She was like a picture on the chocolate box,
So pretty and sweet was she,
And her manner was so loving
The way she jumped up on my knee.
Of course she could be very naughty
Ignoring us when we called her name
Waiting instead to be tempted with prawns,
How she enjoyed this expensive game!
We always felt she was Heaven-sent
For she arrived when our spirits were low,
Her gentle presence brought us the comfort
Which all cat lovers will surely know.
That God should send Mopsy to us
When we needed each other's care
Is one of the wonderful things that He does,
A precious memory now which we share.
God's beautiful creatures enrich our lives
We must protect them from neglect and harm.
We thank Him so much for the gift of Mopsy,
Her funny ways and exquisite charm.

Marigold Benbough

My Endless Love

At sixteen years old I married the most wonderful man on earth,
Along came our Golden wedding day,
We held hands across the hospital bed
We kissed knowing it would not be long
Before our final parting came
For fifty years we had love, laugh and shared our dreams,
How could it end this way?
Cancer has no respect for love or age
He knew his time was near,
He whispered 'Goodbye darling, I love you,'
This nearly made me cry.
He didn't want me to be unhappy,
We knew in heaven we would meet by and by,
Ten years have passed and my new companion is,
Such a lovely little Chihuahua dog,
We love and understand each other
Should I be feeling ill or sad,
No need to say a word,
He's on my lap or sits on the chair by my side,
No matter who should call,
He will not move for anyone
No matter what they do
He's my protector, companion and friend
Our love is really grand.

Mary Parish

Hot Dog!

I whose nature's sop an' flapsome,
Crammed up in this little Datsun,
Wish you'd let me out, you oughta,
Pinin' for a drop o' water.

Don't mind me, I'm just the dog, sir,
Waitin' for me slowsome chauffeur,
Barkin' to you folks who's lookin'
Lemme out, I'm almost cookin'.

I whose fleet, an' sleek an' fast,
Contend with heat, I must outlast!
Me spirits sink, when once had soared,
Me paws burn on the black dashboard.

O' where is 'e? 'As 'e forgot?
As 'e left me here to rot?
After treatin' him so royal,
Haven't I bin always loyal?

The sun 'as surely bleached me hair,
an' 'ere 'e comes without a care,
Steppin' in with welcome breeze,
Unaware of me ill-ease.

The wind is whippin' through the winder,
Kindling me from 'mongst the cinders,
Feel like I've bin in a fire,
Never was me thirst so dire.

I whose troubles go unheard,
For lack do I yer magic words,
But if I could, I'd tell 'im wot,
ck!~#!❭ x✗✍☀ Locked in this Datsun, blinkin' *Hot!*

Gemma Gill

Sweet Susie

She was huddled there in a basket
Shivering really feeling so unsure
Hello little miss, what's your name?
Can I stroke you, would you mind?
You're so sweet, can I take you home?
My, those big eyes they tell it all
Mommy please, she's really cute.

But, my son, she seems so sad
Okay tuck her under your coat
We're home little lass, don't be afraid
Here's your basket warm so snug
Mom, Susie won't eat, what shall we do?
Raw eggs mixed with warm milk

My, how she laps it all up
There, there, shy little lady, glossy black
You've nothing to fear, you're perfectly safe
It's 3.30 early morning, hearing her cries
Down to kitchen, 'Hey, what's amiss?
Are you lonely, missing your mommy?'
Fill a hot-water bottle, water just tepid.

Put in clock, oh yes, soft squeaky toy
Should I roll up newspaper as a threat
Back to bed stagger, so tired
All's quiet, she must be settled
Good morning, sweet puppy, my what's that?
Poo in the corner under my feet it's wet
There, little black face, it's okay
You're a perfect little puppy in every way.

Ann Hathaway

Sam

A young hibiscus grows now on your grave
I note its cry for water and comply
I do not look too long at silver leaves
Or blooms far bluer than the sky

For I must hurry on
There is so much to do
When all is said and done
I should be over you

But it was here that you lay patiently
Watching as I trimmed the grass
Waiting for a word thrown carelessly
Tail wagging as I'd pass

You were my dog my friend,
My good companion
And though I know that you are gone
I feel you waiting for me, silently
Still lying in the sun.

Dilly Parker

Sasha

*(In loving memory of Sasha, family pet Labrador
who sadly passed away in April 1997)*

My Andrex puppy
You were so
Bright and bubbly
In every paw.

You would lick my face
Until your mouth went dry
But you would happily eat
One of Mamma Wray's pies.

You were my best friend
Until the dying end
My little fluffy ball
You liked to chew through the wall.

You would beg politely
And never bite
I will miss you sadly
Because I can't hold you tight.

Goodbye sweet Sasha
You will stay in my heart
Be happy in Doggy Heaven
Until we meet up above.

Tracey Jean Wray

Flossie

Only a stray when we met,
'It was love at first sight',
You a gentle, meek, timid creature,
Always anticipating some mistreatment,
Just seeking any kindness we might give,
Doing everything you could to please us.

Then gradually as you learnt to trust,
Your confidence and character blossomed,
Hours spent together walking and talking,
Miles and smiles over fields and downs,
From badger-watching deep in the woods,
To wading in our pond to 'snap the water'.

The watchful eye kept as we gardened,
A warning bark if strangers came around,
Your gentleness and love of 'Splodge' our cat,
Half of the settee claimed as your favourite bed,
Tolerance of youngsters at 'The Minstead Project',
The difference that you made to their lives.

The total submission when you lay on your back,
The lick of your tongue, a touch from your paw,
A windmilling tail often showing your pleasure,
Magic circles that you made to entertain us all,
'Flossie', you gave love, so many happy memories,
That we will treasure and keep for ever and ever.

David, Jill and Kerry New xx

David J Newman

Sonya

My loving kind and gentle pet,
She's been my friend since she was born,
A smile from me she always gets,
And knows when I'm forlorn.

Her love is unconditional,
And heart is full of fun,
An energy that's unstoppable,
She's loved by everyone.

She's been befriended by our rabbit,
And hounded by a tit,
But she's my one and only habit
That I never want to quit.

A good and faithful Boxer,
And very special friend,
I couldn't do without her,
I love her to no end.

Nikki Robinson

Matty

When I stroke our dog who's just turned five,
I'm filled with wonder how she could survive
those six months in quarantine in the cold,
bleak field, clanging with wires and iron bars.

I can still feel her eyes nailed upon us
through a slit in the crate as she was driven away
by the van to the airport without knowing
what awaited her at the other end
or at the end of all her waiting. Or
did she know? How else could she have survived?

The day came to fetch her and we were bursting
with the anticipation of her shooting at us.
But for a few seconds she could not rise.
Yet, once out of the car, how she pulled us
by the leash towards her new home, and hardly
could contain herself till the door was opened!

Michiko Matthews

Poem For A Pet

Brown dog lying in a patch of sun,
Warm skin, warm fur, warm heart,
A wagging tail when the day is done,
A wag for the new day to start.

Sad dog watching the two of us go,
Head down, big eyes looking on,
Perhaps a deep sigh, a droop of the nose,
Sadder still when we have gone.

Happy dog hearing a key in the door,
Excitedly waiting for someone to come,
Leaping up from your bed on the floor,
Standing erect, eyes bright once more.

Ecstatic dog seeing your lead appear,
Jumping with joy and circling around,
Drawing ever nearer and nearer
Until the door opens and out you bound.

Older dog now, not moving so fast,
Sitting thinking of times that have passed,
What do you dream when your day is done?
Brown dog lying in a patch of sun.

Denise Jones

A Sheeple-Iple

My dog's a Sheeple-iple
A rather unusual breed,
With a heart of gold, but a mind of her own -
Who isn't too good on the lead!
She's a gorgeous little dog
With warm brown eyes and beard
And 'beetley' little eyebrows -
But do not be afeared . . .
If you happen to ring our doorbell
And a savage barking you hear,
She's only doing her duty -
I must make that quite clear.
If you haven't met this breed before,
Sheeple-iple's the name
And when you walk her on the lead
She'll start her little game -
With nose on ground she picks up scent
Of motley offending canines
And frantically *she pulls* me along
Sniffing for telltale signs!
I pull her back with a tug of the lead
As if, any notice she'll take!
I wish I'd trained her as a pup
For everybody's sake!
And so we continue our tug-of-war
She pulls and *I pulls* the game
I love her of course, but now you know
Just how she gets her name!

Elizabeth Scholes

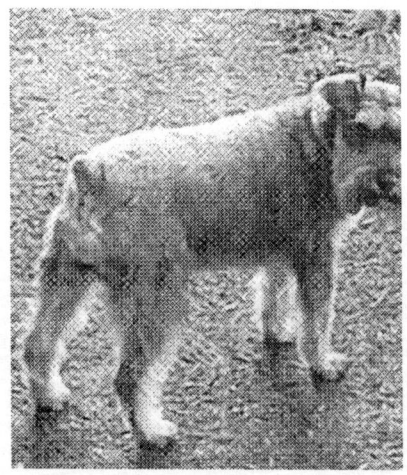

My Cats

My cats,
They are my Monet garden,
My Water Lily pond,
With many shades of black and grey
And snowy-white, and ginger,
And different textures
And reflecting lights
From flashing, tempered eyes.

Is it the eyes
Or is it the coat,
Or just the essence of them
That draws me in . . .
To their depths,
And yet . . . keeps me always
At a surface levelled.

I could paint and paint
Word pictures of my cats,
Yet be no closer to
The inside of their heads
Than I could split the atoms
Of the H_2O
Of the Water Lily Pond.

Margaret Boles

My Dog Ben

My best friend, whose name is Ben,
Was a gift to me when I was ten.
He has quite the nicest nature I know;
Any sign of bad temper he'd never show.

He came to me from a very sad home;
He was so thin you could nearly see bone.
Now he's big and well and strong:
That didn't take him very long.

With a lot of love and some good food too,
Now he's quite as good as new.
He's a black gleaming coat and intelligent eyes;
I know that he is very wise.

When we wake in the morning we go for a walk,
And together we just talk and talk.
Then it's home for breakfast at eight,
And off to school: I mustn't be late!

He stays with Mum while I study each day;
I say: 'Be good while I'm away!'
He loves my mum and my family,
But I'm his boss - that's our destiny.

When I return we have such fun:
He knows at four we're off for a run;
Then it's tea, a drink and a game,
But on Monday it's not the same:

This is the day we go to classes,
And now Ben's behaviour quite surpasses
The early days when he was young,
And training hadn't then begun.

One day my mum was ill and alone,
So Ben knocked down the telephone,
Just enabling her to say;
Please come and help me straightaway!'

Only those who have ever known
A doggy friend of their very own
Know, even if a word's not spoken,
There's a bond that can't be broken.

Jenny Skinner

My Dog Sabre

My dog Sabre
Such a lovely dog he is
He's a collie
Sabre has such a lovely coat
Of light and dark brown fur
With a lovely white mane
He loves to have his paw shaked
Sabre also, like any other dog
Loves to have his tummy tickled
Also loves to go for walkies
He's fifteen years old now
Sabre's still lively for his age
He loves his milk and his
Pedigree Chum and his doggy treats
He always lets you know
When someone comes to the door
He's a good guard dog
He's always alert
Sabre loves being fussed
Sometimes when he'd been naughty
He'd give you that little crafty look
As if to say 'I didn't do it.'
Sabre loves to chase after his tail
He also loves to play with his doggy toys
As soon as you see him you'll just
Fall in love with him.
I love my dog Sabre,
When he dies, I'll miss him.

Stuart Trevaskiss

Horses

I love to see horses running wild in the fields,
No restraint or harnesses, oh the freedom they must feel.
They roll on their backs, chew at grass all day,
When you try to catch them, they gallop away.
They can be naughty, they can be nice,
They're always alert, and so full of life,
They like to go jumping at shows, and be preened
Before judges, best manners is what we like to be seen.
Like to wear their coats when they are cold,
And their saddles and reins, for you to hold.
They like their tails and manes well plaited,
Don't like their hair all knotted and matted.
Like to be groomed and washed, all nice and clean,
When standing in the sun, you can see the gloss and sheen.
Even better, like to be free in the field,
Have the cobbler call, to be shoed and heeled.
Then love to go out and get dirty again,
To get cleaned up once more, exactly the same.

Beverley Diana Burcham

Cosmo

My hamster was only a month old when he died
And that was the day when I cried and cried
He was so friendly and so much fun
He would bring smiles to everyone.
On the day that he died, I woke up in bed
To hear the terrible news that my mum said
I was shocked and wondered what was in store
When I walked downstairs and looked by the door.
He was lying there as if he was asleep
And all I did was sit there and weep and weep and weep.

Sabria Ragab

The Black Cat

Thank you for asking 'Will you take
The black one home to Pembrokeshire?'
'No!' So he came back in a box
Along the motorway in record time
At barely six weeks old.

As rains in rivers lose themselves
And fatten streams, Preseli dark
Is fed upon his polished black;
Only the eyes that are not gold
Or green, but somewhere tawny in-between,
Show us he waits upon the kitchen sill,
Voleful and waxed by night.

First cat of greeting at the gate,
In garden and among the beans,
Your heart is bigger than Wales; hold
That splendid tail, the banner of your love,
Aloft through all the world.

Marianne Whitelaw

The Parrot's Tail

The glories of the east,
Light my heart before my eyes,
The luscious shades of green,
A backdrop of exotics,
For reds and yellows peeping,
From these gorgeous trees,
Displayed on the many varied birds,
That inhabit glorious sections of our globe,
Shimmering streams of blue and silver,
Water enlivened by sun's rays,
Which is forever bringing, shining,
A glow upon the whole scene,
Even when the storm clouds gather,
The coloured scene below, never disappears,
Just a different facet of the scene,
So is God's love for us, no matter,
What the weather of our souls, He,
Does not take hope's colour from our hearts,
As the parrot's tail ne'er grows grey.

Anne Mary McMullan

Pepè (Your Daddy Loves You)

The words are not yet invented,
To express what you mean to me,
So we speak not with words, but with gestures,
To show love and sincerity,

We have our own special language,
That only the two of us know,
With a nod, or a wink, or expression,
Our feelings, the two of us show.

We sit, and we talk for hours,
Without ever saying a word,
Communicating, in total silence,
But every meaning is shared.

You read all my moods and emotions,
And I know just how you feel,
You react to my highs, and my low points,
With friendship, to true, and so real.

More than a pet, you're a soul mate!
You truly are, this man's best friend,
Ever present, and loyal, and faithful,
On you, I can always depend.

My constant, canine, companion,
In everything that I do,
I dedicate this ode, to you Pepè,
To say that, *Your daddy loves you!*'

R S Strong

Dunstan

Had him from being a kitten
Wasn't nothing much but fur
With two round eyes of green
And a midget mew.

Now he is always up to his antics
Walks the neighbouring gardens
Getting up to mischief in the field of gold
Happily playing in his own world.

My Dunstan is a loveable pet
Showing off his white bib and paws
He looks very attractive
With loving kindness.

He purrs contented while being stroked
Eyeballs starting to close
He then drops off to sleep
Accepting all the comforts he needs.

Heather Aspinall

Grandpa's Friend Tim

The cat next door is here again,
I'll have to chase him off
But it's such an effort nowadays
I find it very tough.
I've had my usual walk around
To calculate my leap,
But once I've had my breakfast,
I just want to go to sleep.

They say I have white ears and beard
Although I was once black,
So I must be getting older
As my body feels quite slack,
My master seems to love me
Though he is older too:
We spend more time together,
He has nothing much to do.

He knows where he can find me,
I am sleeping in the shade,
We sit together quietly
Where once we often played.
We keep each other company,
Though we are getting slow,
I can no longer do the tricks
He taught me long ago.

But we understand each other,
And when it's time to part,
We know we'll always have a place
In one another's heart.

I Goldsmith

Selina

Why is it, when I sit down to relax,
And think I'll plan my week, or read awhile,
You clamber on my lap and want a game?
My book goes flying as you nestle down;
Claws pierce my thighs, and as you turn, three times,
Your tail assaults my nose, like old men's snuff,
Before you curl up, where the book once lay.

Just when I think you've settled, one soft paw
Demands attention, tapping on my arm.
I stroke, and tickle; see your green eyes glow
Half closed in bliss. Contentedly, you purr.

I'm flattered by your love; your sleek, warm coat
Caresses me . . . but, should I dare to move,
All changes, and my darling, docile cat
Becomes a spitting, hissing, scratching witch,
And shows the fickle, female feline heart!

Yvonye M Fee

Grace

Gentle, undemanding friendship
    is the gift a dog will bring.
But for food, and warmth and shelter,
    asking not a single thing.
Grace knows when I'm feeling lonely,
    brings me solace to my heart.
Silent sympathy abounding,
    when from friends I've had to part.
Never bearing bitter grudges
    if those words of anger spill,
Just returns to press against me,
    gives me love my heart to fill.
Eyes of liquid honey gazing,
    rapt attention on my face.
Loving, trusting, head now resting,
    the inspiration that is Grace.

Olwyn Green

Lucky Black Cat

Let me introduce myself, my name is *Bertie Edge*
There's nothing I like better than sitting on the window ledge,
Watching out for predators encroaching on my garden,
If other cats should dare to, then they have to beg my pardon.

I am dark and sleek and handsome,
Some say that I'm proud and haughty,
And if I'm bored on rainy days
Then I can be a little naughty.

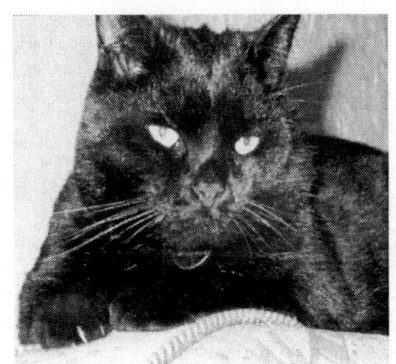

I am very clean and particular
And I'm choosy about what I eat.
My favourite food is biscuits
But I also like chicken and meat.

I always have someone at home with me,
My dad is retired you see.
He is devoted to me, as I am to him
And he gives me a life of luxury.

I love my mum, but there's one thing wrong,
She wants to pick me up and stroke me.
She knows I don't like that sort of thing
And I have to nip her sometimes to get free.

To help me get in and out of the house
A cat flap was bought from the store.
But if I rattle the flap using my paw
My dad comes to open the door.

I know that I'm pampered and very lucky
To live with a family like mine,
And if this can continue for the rest of my days
Then that will suit me just fine.

Gillian Edge

Tommy

I lost my pal Bertie after 14 years;
He left me devastated, full of tears;
The house seemed empty, every day;
Life became so void and grey.

Then, the good Lord, to me, did send
Another companion, and loyal friend;
From whence he came, I've not a clue,
He just appeared, *out of the blue*.

Though not a dog, like my departed pet,
I was *hooked* as soon as I met
This handsome tom cat, ginger and white,
Who never wanders far from my sight.

I've called him Tommy, a common name;
One that suits him, all the same;
Although for us it's still early days,
We are quick to learn each other's ways.

He can never replace the one who's gone above,
Yet, to me, he shows the same kind of love;
People give me looks of disbelief and surprise,
When I tell them, *Bertie's back, in another guise!*

Bernice M Grocott

The Gift

My life had almost hit rock bottom
All I wanted was to be forgotten
When, with a box my son walked in,
A surprise for me hidden within.

A ball of fluff and two big bright eyes
Oh what a really wonderful surprise
The cutest kitten I ever did see,
Was sitting there peering up at me.

I carefully lifted him out of the box
He was so small he'd fit into your socks.
With a *squeak* for a miaow, and not yet a purr
And beautiful tabby markings coloured his fur.

As he's grown up over the last year.
He had made us laugh and brought us such cheer
His inquisitive nature, his love of life
He makes you forget all about your strife.

The simplest of things he would have to invest,
And everything you did, he would show interest
If you turned on the taps, gave the toilet a flush
From wherever he was he'd come with a rush.

Tearing up tissues, chasing a ball
Playing up and down stairs with a straw 'til he falls
Pouncing in bags, getting your feet
Laying on the chair near the radiator for heat.

He loves you to chase him, he so loves to play
He just makes us laugh as we watch him each day
From his first step outside, his first paw in the snow
He is always excited, he just loves life so.

So from our kitten so innocent and small
We could laugh again, life's worth living after all
So whatever your troubles, whatever your strife,
Remember the fun, it's a beautiful life.

Denise Jeffcoate

Gelert

Gelert. Ho! Faithful hound, remembered now in every age,
immortalised by Prince Llewellyn's impetuous rage.
Cannine intuition kept you back from joy of hunting with the pack.
Fiendish wolf who came to prey will kill no more,
Wolf's scarlet blood, stains now the palace floor.

Prince Llewellyn returning from the chase,
to see his new born son did haste.
In bloodstained cot no princely child could find,
but bloodstained floor and Gelert's crimson hide,
an impetuous thrust of sword pierced faithful Gelert's side.

That hasty action pierced two hearts that day,
for in the ante-room foul wolf on palace floor, he lay,
and sweet Llewellyn's son, plays on the palace floor,
what bitter grief, our prince will smile no more.

Now lies brave Gilert in Beddgelert fertile ground,
where river Glaslyn makes its joyful sound,
and many travellers come to see his grave
memorial to faithful Gelert, Gelert The Brave.

E L G Holmes

Man's Best Friend

You'll be my eyes sometimes,
You'll even put me on alert
If only people stopped to think
You to hurt.
When you laid your head on my shoulder
Then snuggled your face under my chin
I'll put my arms around you and let the love
Come from within.
Each step you took beside me,
The bond went on and on.
Protection you gave to me,
Yet your life I couldn't save,
It was cancer which was to put you,
In an early grave.
How I wish I could cuddle you,
And say thank you for the love you gave
Thank you should have been said
Before the memories fade.
You'll be my eyes sometimes
You'll even put me on alert,
You'll snuggle your head under my chin
Precious you were to me,
My very precious friend, lots of tongues wagging
Watching your tail rotate was great,
Because I could see you were happy
With the affection I gave to you all that's left to say
Is a big thank you.

Rachel Tahan

Love Unconditional

She never asks a question
And yet she's always there,
Her love is unconditional,
Her love is always fair.

She has no sense of reason,
The time she cannot tell,
But for rising and retiring,
These times she knows quite well.

And then of course there's supper,
She knows she'll get a snack,
Five finger tips of butter
Helps keep her coat gloss black.

When beads of light are dancing
On ceiling or on wall,
She'll jump so high to catch them,
But never will she fall.

She loves to have her comfort,
Security and heat,
When waking in the morning
She's curled up 'round my feet.

Someone to share your problems,
A listening ear to bend,
How could I live without her?
My little feline friend.

Colin Ross

Ma Cat

Soft and smooth ma hand runs over
The back of ma wee friend.
Ah wish that he could talk an tell me
Our love will never end.

He rubs his head up on tae mine
An sits upon ma knee.
Ah pick him up an cuddle him
His only love is me.

He stares at me cause a've tae feed him
Or he'll cry awe day,
But there's a place inside ma heart
Where he will always stay.

He sits upon his basket,
An lies there straight out flat.
Ah wonder what he's thinking,
Cause he's ma only cat.

James Lunan

The Blackbird

Flash! There he goes,
Blackbird in my tree!
Every day he comes,
Must be other creatures
I can't see outside,
I'm watching from my window
As he sits there astride
The branches, looking
For the, to me, invisible bugs
That must be in my tree.
He stays a little while
And satisfies his urge
Then flits away as quick
As a momentary flick
Of the pages in my book.
Tomorrow he'll come again,
Sun, wind, snow or rain,
He'll be there, sure as sure,
A creature of habit come
To search for more invisible
To me, bugs that must be in my tree.

Joan Blissett

A Tribute To Gino My Faithful Dog

There was a dog called Gino
Black and tan
With a white mane
A super fantastic dog he was
My dog he was
Born 13th September 1979
Died 31st of July 1997
18 years old he was
My loveable faithful dog
Many a star name he met
Barbara Woodhouse, Lord Patrick Lichfield,
Lynette McMorrough,
To name but some
I love and loved my dog Gino
He's now in doggy heaven
My loveable faithful dog
Gino Giovanni, flycatcher hall.

David J Hall

Happiness

White high ceilinged, fresh and cool,
A place I come to as a rule
When tired, or weary, sad or blue
My cool white bedroom, I come to you
To lay me down on your smooth white bed
And on the soft pillow lay my head.
To there relax, and be at peace
Is, for me, a great release - of tension.

And then the sun comes filtering in
Through muslin net, soft and dim
My dog Amy lies and pants awhile,
Tuppy the cat on my chest as on a stile;
And pant and purr and sun streams in
With the cat's big smile and the dog's happy grin,
Soon I'm up and about, and happy again.

Rose-Mary Oskam-Clark

Trudy

Big, brown eyes
Gazing softly down at me.
Trusting and caring
Sharing many triumphs.

A special link
That connects us together,
To become a pair
And gain a strong trust.

Her fluffy winter coat,
Her distinguishing white face
Pricked up ears,
And her dopey expressions,
I love her.

Francesca Ellison

Canine Friends

Patsy's coat was that of a pointer, all the spots were in the right place.
But her dad had been an Alsation (her mum had definitely fallen from grace).
She was loving and trustful and patient, always on duty right there at my side.
No stranger could enter to harm me, she'd just look and they stayed right outside.

Rex was ten years of age when we got her, an eight week old bundle of fur,
But she stole his old heart in an instant, if he'd been a cat he'd have purred.
As old age overtook him, he faltered, first he went deaf and then blind,
But Patsy watched o'er him and loved him, she never let him get left behind,
With his lead in her mouth she would lead him, over the fields near our home,
And when he slept she would lie down beside him, not once did she leave him alone.

Then he died and her heart it was broken, no more did her tail wag with joy.
She just lay in her basket and whimpered, for Rex, her own darling boy.
Now she too has made that last journey, and I'd like to think (No I know).
That old Rex, fit and well ran to greet her, saying
Oh Patsy, I have missed you so!

Barbara Glennon

Little Rascal (To Oscar Little Rascal)

You're only a little tiny dog
Full of mischief and devil my care.
You only bark to let us know you
Are there. You wake us up to see if we
Are alive. With a lick on the cheek
And wag of your tail, you're hot on
The trail to make us play
With toys and anything you can pinch.
You love to snarl and bark and hid
Your spoils, all the mail, it's straight
In your basket, you guarding it with all your might.
When you let us have our belongings back
You're straight to the door looking for more.
You think everyone is coming to the house
And guard it with all your cunning.
But bless you I wouldn't be without you.
My little monster, we all love you so much.

Joan Finn

My Song To A Dog

The life of a dog is not very long
But this is my song to a dog who is gone
To the great paws above
Who will cuddle and give
Lots of presents to my dog
Who knew how to live.

For she greeted me daily
With smiles and a jump

And whatever I did
She would waggle her stump.

For her tail it was short
But her heart it was bold
And the great love within it
Did never run cold.

Michela St Lo Beckett

Mister Insey

We haven't got a cat
And we haven't got a dog,
We haven't got a rabbit
And we haven't got a frog!

We haven't got a gerbil,
Nor have we got a mouse,
Not even a goldfish in a bowl
Living in our house.

But often after dinner,
When the curtains are all drawn,
The fire is lit, a soft light shines,
It's cosy and it's warm.

A tiny little spider
Comes scampering across the floor,
It stops a while, then scampers on,
Heading for the door.

He's a friendly little creature.
He doesn't mean any harm,
So all I do is sit very still,
And do my best to stay calm!

I would never hurt him
For he is so small,
Dashing to the safety
Of our tiny hall.

I have heard some people say,
As strange as it may seem,
Spiders will only choose a home
That's warm and safe and clean.

Sylvia A Whitaker

The Web Site

We have a new pet in the house
It isn't a rabbit, a dog or a mouse
He arrived uninvited and lodges rent free
His home is a corner behind the TV
With very long legs and a body that's hairy
He's a creepy crawly whose rather scary
Flies he captures and creatures like that
But is rather wary of Lucy our cat
He's not at all cuddly
And doesn't play with toys
He's big and deadly and makes no noise.

Neighbours call and get quite a scare
Sometimes they scream and jump on the chair
He's quiet all day and lively at night
When he runs up the curtains
It gives them a fright.

Where he came from we just don't know
Into the garden he had to go
Our unwelcome guest we'll see no more.

Oh no! Who did I just see, creep under the door!

Lilian France

Pharaoh Cat

Pharaoh cat, cat of my dreams,
Black fur gleaming, golden eyes staring.
Egyptian dreams, we have been sharing,
Elusive yet near, distant but caring.
How come you know me, how
Come you are sharing,
Down through the centuries, love's
Light shining, always our souls
For ever entwining.

Regal, handsome, proud and aloof,
Your spirit wild, but dignified,
I couldn't tame you if I wanted too.
Did your ancestors live in the temples?
Did they serve the Egyptian kings
Or were they too thought to be sacred
And allowed to roam, and be free?
Pharaoh cat, cat of the kings
Black fur gleaming, golden eyes staring
Egyptian dreams, we have been sharing.

Eileen M Shapcott

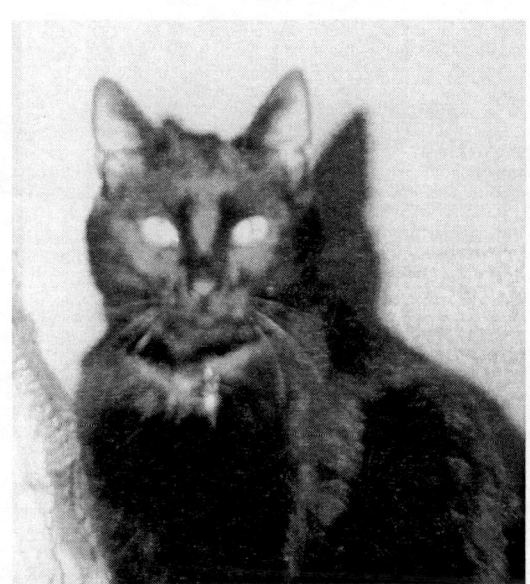

Ode To Dinky

They walk across the fields,
Martin and little dog Dinky,
She looks so sweet, so sedate,
As if butter would not melt on her plate,
Woe betide any canine male - she will
Put the wind in his sail.

Any dog going near her master, will
Surely be courting some disaster.
With rabbits for tea, run rabbit run
Or you'll end up in Dinky's tum.
So together they walk come rain
Or come shine, taking the air as if
It were wine.

Jean Fox

Matthew

A being unique, not special, spare
posture betraying loneliness, soul aching care.
Some moments companionship brightens weary hours,
awareness of pain seeds compassionate flowers.

Spoken word denied you, every line reflects
the inner pain of aloneness, even despair, I suspect.
No matter, connection has multi-facets
soul suffering lessened, suddenly bright aspects.

I talk, you hiccup and blink.
Method of communication unimportant, I think.
Reaching out to another, the impulse, the goal.
The truest bonding comes direct from the soul.

Interaction of value needs little thought,
kinship develops I chatter, you retort.
Friendship now beginning, expectations awake,
I tease, you're disdainful, now fears abate.

A woman, another, both creatures afloat,
strange pairing, our emotion, heats like a coat.
Interest, sharing, the caring self,
A donkey friend's warmth cuddling coals of wealth.

Patricia Lynwood

Polly

I love you my Pol:
You are my best friend -
We walk together in rain and shine
And have that special feeling
For one another
That no one would understand
Unless they know you and were alone.

I love you my friend.
I'll always be there for you
As you have been for me
A lick, a kiss, a wag,
You wait patiently for my return
When I cannot take you
And greet me so warmly when I return.

You make my house a home
You make me feel needed
I'm so glad you are here with me
I don't know how I'd manage
If you were to go.

I love you my Pol . . .
My thanks for the love and the
Happiness you've given to me.
I wouldn't have missed knowing you
For the world.
Your loyalty is precious
More than ever a *human being* can give
You are my Yorkie, my Polly,
I love you.

Mary Williamson

A Change Of Heart

No, you can't have a cat, I said no!
Just forget all about it, now go.
I just don't want a cat in the house,
No, even though it may catch me a mouse.
Now forget it, it just isn't on,
Yes I know that you kids both want one,
But me and your dad both say no,
That's the end of the story, just go.

Oh, just ask your dad, I'm fed up
No you certainly can't have a pup
He said yes, well he must have been drunk,
Oh he was, why the traitor, the skunk.
Well I won't have a cat in the house,
Even though it may catch me a mouse.

Aah it's Ginger, a female or tom?
But to keep it would cost me a bomb,
Yes she's sweet, but she cannot live here,
Her injections and things are too dear.
Give her something to play with - a mitten,
After all she is only a kitten.
Now Jayne, you must buy her a tray,
And a collar in case she should stray,
But for now she can sleep on my bed,
All right I know what I said.
But I love her already, she's cute,
But I think I'll give daddy the boot!

Eileen Burton

Dani's Pal Rupert

This is my pal Rupert
he comes to visit me once in a while
lives with my Nana and Grandad
and he always makes me smile.

I love to give him cuddles
and biscuits from his bowl
take him on long walks
or in the countryside for a stroll.

He chases all the sticks I throw
noisily barking as he goes
his favourite treat is chocolate
or ice cream from my cone.

We love to wonder in the woodlands
and sniff at all the scented flowers
or go to the park together
were we could spend just hours.

We often bounce a ball between us
or splash in the paddling pool
and he loves to come and meet me
when I come out from my play school.

He lets me lie upon him
or cover with a cosy quilt
dress him in my favourite T-shirt
or brush him till his coat's like silk.

I know he is my pal
as he licks me on my cheek
he never tugs me as I hold his lead
and lets me snuggle near him while we both sleep.

Christina B Cox

Kara

She had two strokes, she scarce could turn her head,
But gamely lolloped after us short way across the field.
It didn't last, we knew it couldn't last.
She was so sick and old but brave and game and loving to the end.

The brown eyes said, *I trust you, whatever you think best*
Is right for me. (Would God that I could say as much to him!)
And so she went, slipped out into the dark, to find the light
Of some unending puppy hood, joyous and free, with friends who've gone before.
And one day she'll come bounding up again, paws pushing with delight,
As we, her human friends, reach that eternal shore.

Sr E Morris

My Cat

You are cat;
Graceful: elegant and distant.
And you are cat;
Cunning: mischievous: confident.
You are master,
Not mastered.
A king among kings;
The prince of thieves.
You are cat;
Nimble, tactile and mild.
And you are cat;
Discreet: territorial; wild.
You are cat.
Just silly old cat.
My cat;
A friend for life.

Marcus Tyler

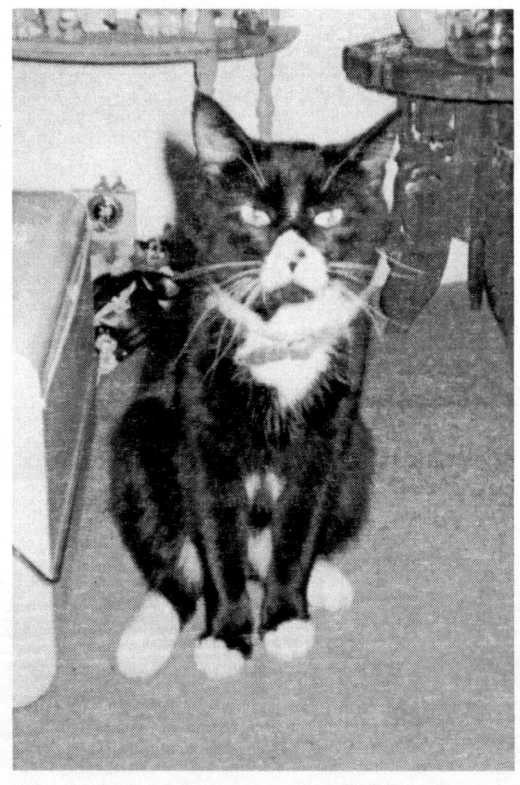

Golden Dog

With a mane of gold today
Tomorrow, murky brown
Then you bark and run,
To your warm and cosy den.

Your brown eyes look for attention,
In the place you call your home
Waging your tail in full display,
Of the joy you feel within.

Your golden mane falls in place,
As you lift your head
To the call of your name
Hoping in vain,
For a treat to come.

Carol Gilby

Feline Magic

White feline beauty
sleeping on chair
what care you for my world.
You . . . eat . . . sleep wander
all over house and garden
where your every whim is
fulfilled, of course you
bring petty disorder sometimes
when destruction with sharp
claws is your want or
flattening prize plants in a
daily chase of birds and
butterflies, but, when I
am tired or in despair
up on my lap a healing
spirit nestles there, then
the soft gentle purr plus
the warm silvery coat and
beating of a companion
heart, makes me realise
how dull was my life
without the quiet pleasure,
of stroking, your smooth
silky fur at the close
of my world's hectic day.

H A Brawn-Meek

Tigger

It is a scorching morning,
In early summer '99,
The sun is just rising,
How on earth could I
Haul myself up from my cosy nest?

I trundle downstairs, still half asleep
A voice says cheerfully
Wake up sleepy head, remember,
Today we're getting a cat!

Excitedly, I start to dress,
But soon wish I had not
I have odd socks, my hair's a mess
My jumper is on inside out.

As we approach the rescue centre
I begin to think of names,
I see the one I want,
She's orange, ginger and white,
With a little pink nose.

The perfect name is . . . Tigger!

Holly Evans

The Alpha And Omega He

From chrysalis to butterfly . . . I love lettuce!

Me, earthly, yet
　　　thanks for my being
My youth is ageing
　　　Almost unnoticeable.

　　　I feel slower
　　　A little lower too -
　　　Fading I think -
In my cocooned body. (the outward shell)

A deep sense of me
　　　Emerges, shedding this coat
　　　And leaving a winged soul
　　　Thus setting it free
　　　Into the ether
　　　Suffice to flutter
Thro' to eternity on wings of immortality . . .

　　　And I am grateful, Lord
　　　For thinking of me.
In the beginning and at the end, I hope I've been true
　　　In what you destined me to do.

Kathleen Mould

My Dog Sheba

My dog Sheba
Such a lovely dog she is
She's a collie cross
Sheba's 9 years old now
She's such a soft friendly
Affectionate dog.
Sheba always wants a fuss
She's got such a lovely coat
Of soft dark and light brown fur
Sheba loves her doggy chews
She also loves going out for walkies.
Sheba always lets you know
When there's someone at the door
She's always very alert
Sheba's a very good guard dog
Like all other dogs they love
Lots of love and affection and treats
If you're a dog owner then
You'll know what I mean
As soon as you see her
You can't help but like my dog Sheba.
I love her to bits,
I wouldn't want to be
Without my dog Sheba
She loves having her tummy tickled
I'll miss her when she dies.

Michelle Knight

Waiting

While waiting for my dog, Bobby, to be put to sleep.

Dear Bobby, your last hour is passing,
The clock ticks on relentless
In its march of time.
I have often wondered how it would be,
But never thought that it would be like this.
On Kale's anniversary it is
Your turn today, no fuss,
Just gentle acceptance.
The memories flood in, the bad, the good,
Over 16 years you were bad at first but in time
Became my faithful and loving companion.
Treasured memories of thee,
Welcombe Hills of Talybont
Walks over the fields and of other
Happy times,
Go now to your pals, Betsy, Kale and Jet
Rest in peace, under the apple tree,
I will never forget you.

A M Moore

My Hamsters

So small and plump,
Cute and sweet.
Kay Ko and Zippy.

Round and round they go,
So fast at night.
It's fun to watch them run,
So sweet as they wash.

They eat anything that you or I might.
My two little girls,
Hamsters so sweet.

Charlotte Stace

Sadness To Joy

My precious cat was dead and gone
My heart was broken and sad.
For thirteen years she'd been my friend,
She shared my sorrows and my joys,
Always there through good and bad.

A light within my life went out,
The days stretched empty and dark.
My tears I shed upon her grave,
Tokens of flowers for Susie laid,
But still the pain was sharp.

Tho' she could never be replaced,
Rescue homes are full of good
And lonely cats, all needing homes,
Places to call their own again
With love, and warmth, and food.

But how to choose just one new friend
When all were in such need.
Then, tiny face and huge sad eyes,
So small and helpless, there she was -
Our hearts were won indeed.

So Lottie came to ease my pain,
My broken heart to mend.
Tho' Susie in the memory stays,
This lovely little creature lives
Secure to her life's end.

God gave to us this precious gift -
Those eyes no longer sad,
Her fur is soft, her love is true,
We give Him thanks for all she is,
Once more our lives are glad.

Jill Richards

Devon Dogs

A blue eyed, brown eyed border collie
following his somewhat sheepish master,
ineffectual and affectionate
apparently impervious to his
collie colleague's antics
dementedly
attempting to shepherd
the master's Landrover,
exhausted at the rear.

A tufty mud-encrusted Jack Russell
who madly, muddily made our acquaintance.
The liver-coated Springer
so gentle and so shy.
Another collie who trembled
as we ambled peaceably by.

Late lunch highlighted by
Tuffy's rapid return;
our frenzied friend rolling over
to receive his welcome;
a swift removal of cheese
from within range of his enquiring nostrils
and tongue.

These and other snapshots
fill the album of my memory,
capturing forever
the warmth and love
of a seventh heaven -
time with friends in deepest Devon.

Julia Murphy

My Cat

Sleek and shiny black is my cat's coat
Right from a kitten on him I'd dote,
A long swishing tail and very sharp claws
Eyes of amber and teeth like *Jaws*
He'd a roguish character right from the start
But he has a truly affectionate and loving heart
He carries bits and bobs about in his teeth
And if the tin is left open, he's a sweetie thief
Partly chewed sweets I find on the floor
But I can't get angry 'cos it's him I adore
Nothing is safe from his inquisitive eyes
Anything left around becomes his prize.
He seems to enjoy hoarding things down chairs
Watches, baby's socks and tiny teddy bears
He loves being chased, then hides behind a door
He springs out on your feet, then he's off again
As if he's asking for more
And when on the foot of my bed he lies curled
I know I couldn't part with him for all the world.

C D Kettle

My Dogs

Sitting on my bench alone,
In the corner of the lawn,
This small square of grass it seems,
Holds my past of canine dreams.

In the centre lies our Spot,
Good friend to all that lived around.
He liked to stand on neutral ground.
All dogs respected him for that,
Especially his friend the cat.
Seventeen years he travelled on,
And then one day he just was gone.

Spot the second came along,
To fill that empty space.
Strong and purposeful was he,
A stronger swimmer you ne'er did see.
He loved to roam the shore with me,
Back through the fields in the time for tea.
And now he lies at the end of lawn,
Rest in peace, no more to roam.

Patch, she now has passed away,
Twenty years she came to stay.
All through her life she gave us joy,
In the van she loved to ride,
Sitting close, side by side.
That was were she loved to be.
In the border now she lies,
Near the bench among the flowers.
On the bench I love to be,
All my dogs are still with me.

Peter Isles Orr

Terriers

The delights of running free
With the comforting knowledge
Of owner's kindly plodding to the rear
That knowledge checked upon
By hasty, intermittent backward glances.
Now with feet drumming like hooves
Now pausing for super-sensitive sniffing
Then off to root amongst
The leafy labyrinths of a nearby copse.
Brambles and nettles beaten back
Hind legs held high like a rabbit.
Damp air is rich with fir cone smells
With moss and rotting logs and peaty loam
Shattered toadstools, puffballs, old grass cuttings
Little night-time creatures leave their trails
Now here. now there,
And scents of other dogs emerge - compelling and diverse.
A doubtful titbit found and crunched
With clandestine delight.
The thrill of power from closing in
On some beleaguered cat or tripping gull.
Whether being at one with the sun's gleam
Or the sun's chequering
The blasting of the wind
Or challenge of the rain or snow
It's all acceptable
And only whets the appetite for more
Within the dog-deep consciousness
And homeward-bound means only taking rest
To greet the ever-embryonic day.

Norah Mitchell

The Growl

I've got a little car,
Doesn't take me very far,
But as far as I'm concerned it's the thing.
I was going out at night,
Wind and rain and frost in spite,
Then it happened and it made my poor heart sing.

It was getting rather late.
I was going with my date
And we often thought of pussy on the prowl.
But then a strange event
That through my poor heart went.
It was pussy sitting giving out a growl.

Hadn't seen him in the dark.
Dogs would have given a bark
But this cat went and made the softest sound.
Much to my surprise
I saw his yellow eyes
And saw him sitting as I looked around.

Cats are afraid, I'm often told,
But this one really was quite bold.
I gave a gentle pat upon his head
He rubbed against my arm,
Showing he'd not come to harm
And then quickly off into the darkness fled.

Thomas W Splitt

Not My Pet

You would not think that spiders might be pets.
At least, I did not think so, but they can.
　　　　(You never know . . .)

A family friend of mine (she's not so young)
Has one large spider, plump and black, as pet.
　　　　(She's fond of him).

He lives between the curtain and the glass
Of her front door. He weaves. He sleeps.
　　　　(So quiet, so clean).

Now, spiders certainly do their work well:
They're keen, they're so artistic - see their lace
　　　　of shining silk.

I wouldn't choose this scrambling, scowling ghost
For company. But then . . . he might not want
　　　　me either for *his* pet.

And so, we're quits.

Katharine Holmstrom

Doggy Devotion

Nip was his name, we all loved him
A black and tan mongrel, my son's whim
He brought him home saying 'Can he be mine?'
Not certain, but captivated, I said 'Yes, fine.'

The first few weeks were very trying
Up at night every three hours with yelping and crying
A young pup had left his mum and others
We don't know what happened to his brothers.

Life settled down, Nip fitted in well
Games in the field and countryside where we dwell
Shopping in the village trained on a lead
Happily greeting all, oh happy indeed!

Years passed quickly. Nip loved my old mother
He lay on her feet when it was cold weather
They became such good friends day and night
Keeping her safe even at night.

It's very sad to say goodbye to a friend
Age and health meant life had to end
The vet shook his head and said 'It's goodbye.'
When that happened many a tear dimmed my eye.

Bessie Groves

Sabre

He looked at me with doleful eyes
When we said our last goodbyes.
I was losing a dear friend
And knew this was the very end.

We'd run, skipped and jumped around
You made me laugh, my puppy hound.
Always there when I felt sad
Shared my joy when I was glad.

I called you 'Sabre', it suited you
So big and strong, loving too.
You were a clown loved by all
My heart went with you, I'm now so forlorn.

My love for you will never die,
I didn't want to say goodbye.
My darling Alsation you were only eleven.
Rest in peace now that you're in heaven.

Sheila Ryan

My Two Cats

Your big green eyes stare up at me,
Trust and devotion for all to see.
So timid and so very shy,
Hiding from every passer-by.
Venturing out in the dark of night,
But by day you're out of sight.
No-one else could realise,
The love I see within your eyes.
And when I close the house up tight,
You're by my side throughout the night.
Rising too when I have to,
My second shadow that is you.
So different from my other cat,
Who's always doing this and that.
So full of life never off the go,
Fur as white as the driven snow.
Her day is spent having fun,
Admired and petted by everyone.
To choose between you, I could not,
You're all the family that I've got.
Nothing I see I'd change so far
For I love you both the way you are.

M Muirhead

Apple

Slicing segments of apple
With surgical care
I smiled at the pleasure I derive
From giving.

In the garden, he hopped
From perch to perch,
The greens and reds of his feathers
Caught, unashamed, in the sunlight.

Wedging each piece between the bars
I licked the tartness from me,
My tongue flicking around
The circumference of my dry lips.

Easing away, I waited silently
Watching him edge closer,
Peeking down suspiciously
At the exposed underbelly of fruit,
Offered in trapped sacrifice.

The first mouthful was tasted;
Juice smearing the hard shell of beak,
As the ache of pleasure abated
And fulfilment registered on his face.

Soon, the crescent slices were all devoured
As, satisfied,
I slithered away.

Andrew Detheridge

A-Z Of My Pet

A is for his affections
B is for his bark
C is for his name 'Chappie'
D is for his dark eyes
E is for his energy
F is for his floppy ears
G is for his growling
H is for his hairy tail
I is for his intelligence
J is for his jumping
K is his breed, King Charles Spaniel
L is for his little legs
M is for he a mummy's boy
N is for his black nose
O is for his orangy-browny coat
P is for his paws
Q is for he is quiet
R is for his rich coat
S is for his endless snoring
T is for his long tongue
U is for his undercoat
V is for his non-vicious ways
W is for his white fur
X is for his extremely cuddly ways
Y is for his three years of age
Z is for his zany character.

Lisa Martin

Dolly-May

(Poem dedicated to my first pony when I was 14)

A white horse called
Dolly-May
Never called white
But always grey
A 12.2 in hands
Obeyed all commands
Out on a hack
With the tack
Sat astride enjoying
The ride.
Taking note, what's outside
Traffic past, slow and fast.
Steady girl, get on the grass
Riding out for over one hour.
Let's now head for home,
My little flower
I see, home in sight.
Let's be home soon,
Untack Dolly-May
While she nibbles on her
Hay.

Caroline-Janney

Daisy

I'm often like a scarecrow when gardening in the wind,
Muddy shoes and ladders from thorns and prickly things.
Hair all awry, black hands with bleeding scratches
Old clothes are warm but nothing really matches
But how I look won't matter for all that bothers her
Is that I stop and have a word in answer to her purr.

There's times I'm late from shopping and the rain begins to fall
But I always find her waiting with patience on the wall
With not a word of criticism - just her own special call.

My lap which is her favourite place is often occupied with wool
And pins and books and things but purring still she says
'I only need a tiny patch, my head is very neat
And legs and tail and rest of me can squeeze down on the seat.'

She smells my fish and well I know she'd love to have a bite
So few white flakes are then transferred to her own special plate.
A little drop of cream sometimes will fill her with delight
And a soft warm cushion on the chair is her resting place at night.

When sudden noise of thunder or something quite unknown
Fills her with fright, I hold her tight 'til the nasty thing has gone.
If everyone loved everyone as Daisy and I do
The world would be a happier place and quarrelling be taboo.

Phyllis Moore

Tabitha

Hi! My name is Tabitha
I'm a diabetic cat
I can't go out to play anymore
But I've accepted that.

My mum gives me the needle
Each morning and at night
I didn't like it much at first
It gave me quite a fright.

Food-wise it's very uninteresting
No cat meat, fish or such.
I have the dry food variety
Which I don't like very much.

But on the plus side of life
I travel many miles
When 'Mum' visits her friends
You should see the people smile.

I travel by the car, also by the train
If the weather is sunny,
Even if it rains.

So all you diabetic cats out there
Beware and please take heed.
You'll get some funny looks
When you go walkies on a lead.

Yvonne Lewis

Dalmations

Dalmations, what can you say about Dalmations?
If you had one, no explanations
Clean elegant brown languid eyes
Loyal trusting, that's not lies
I could be crying without a sound
As sure as fate over she'd bound
Instinctively knowing all was not well
Transmitting my thoughts she could tell.

You can't put time on something so precious
Without saying they get the message
My first name Charie was fair of face
My second Topsy I could never replace
Two females so loving and true
I now have a dog sparkling new
All the way from Ireland, a bit of a joke
I should have known as he is a bloke.

Poor old Topsy nearly fourteen
She's still the boss and licks him clean
Large and handsome full of tricks
He sussed me out and picked my wits
From a playful pup who ran away
Another loyal dog in his way
Understanding animals, using tact
He knows exactly who leads the pack . . .

Jean Tennent Mitchell

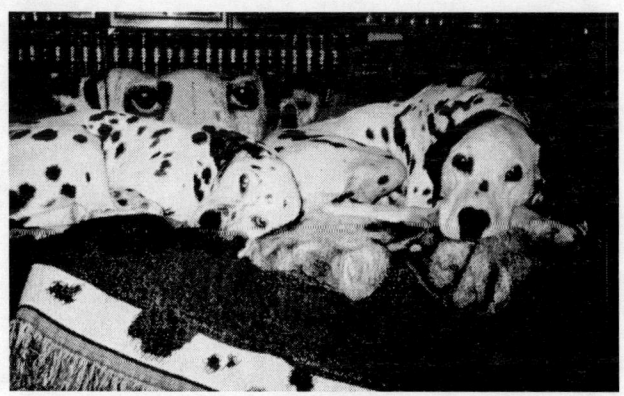

Our Cat

Our cat has a habit
Of sleeping for hours on end,
Then going back
To sleep some more.

Our cat has a habit
Of eating spiders,
(quite disgusting).

Our cat has a habit
Of being selectively deaf,
And only hearing when *he* wants to.

Our cat has a habit
Of pouncing on snowflakes,
As if they were mice.

Our cat has a habit
Of watching nature programmes on TV,
(especially ones about birds).

Our cat has a habit
Of visiting a cat friend
Down our road,
And eating all her dinner.

Our cat has a habit
Of leaving goldfish on our front drive.
(Sorry if they're yours).

I suppose he's a pretty normal cat really.

Melanie Amegatse

All Right Jack!

A playful pose,
A cold wet nose.
Adoring glances
Pranks and prances.
Constant shadow
Following me.

Rings and balls and bones
Litter the floor, and moans
Emit when I stub my toe.
A look of guilt but not for long,
Let's play a game, let's sing a song.
We're friends again - let's go!

Naughty spells,
Funny smells.
Evening cuddles,
Unwelcome puddles.
Walks in the country
And so much more:

Someone to tell my secrets to.
Unbiased and loving people are few
But who needs them: unable to be
As loyal and trusting as you, to me.
You're tough - I'm sentimental,
Happy to know you - Jack Russell.

Brenda Dove

Ode To Penelope

'Penelope, Penelope, wherefore art thou my guinea pig?
Have you buried yourself on an 'adventure dig?'
Are you under the hay or tucked up in your bed?
At last I hear your delighted squeak, I spy your furry head!

I have here a feast for you to devour,
Delicious carrots and nutritious cauliflower
All chopped and sliced up in your personal cup,
So come along and eat it all up!

With your cheeky face and spiky crest
You are by far and away simply the best!
Although you can be stubborn and wilful
Your hops, jumps and grunts are awesomely skilful!

Your high-pitched squeaky greeting brightens my day,
Though you're sometimes moody I wouldn't want you any other way.
I will love you forever my cuddly Penelope
You're the only guinea pig for me!

Emiline McLaughlin

Fluffy Friend

His coat is gold and glossy and ruffles when he curls
His eyes are bright and hazel and sparkle like two pearls
His nose is cold and black and wet which tells you he is well
His velvet tongue is long and pink, he's crafty you can tell
His little paws are small and neat, his nails are short and brittle
He's got a cheeky, loving face, he's round and plump and little
His tail is long and fluffy and moves from side to side
Which shows you he is happy and full of bouncing pride
To watch him play is such a treat, I love him so I'm glad he's mine
His little bark makes him complete, I want him with me all the time
He'll always be close by my side, forever, till the end
He'll always mean so much to me, my special fluffy friend.

S Brown

Pet Heaven

Beautiful dreamer,
Beautiful girl,
Queen of your canine world;
Eager companion on first light forays
And glorious autumn days;
Crunching the crisp golden leaves,
Braving the bitter winter breeze;
Greedily sniffing the fresh scent of spring,
Suffering the prickly heat the summers bring.

Beautiful dreamer,
Beautiful girl;
Coat as black as the enveloping night,
Eyes as sharp as an eagle's sight;
Ears pointed like a hunting wolf,
Panting wet tongue whose kisses engulf;
Even while we sleep we're never far apart,
Such courage and grace just like a lionheart.

Beautiful dreamer,
Beautiful girl;
I hope that wherever you may be,
You're running, happy and free,
through endless fields of green;
Hunting with your pack,
As in time gone by,
Reaching boldly for the sky.

Patricia M Howard

Free As A Bird

He's still on your shoulder
We let out a roar
As my father got up
To answer the door
But the loud shout
Just gave him a fright
And my pet Lazlo
Flew into the night
'Don't worry he'll turn up'
Comforted my dad
But everything he said
Just made me mad

'This is your fault'
I shouted with rage
'But you are the one
Who let him out of his cage'
So up went the notices
The very next day
Will somebody find him?
All we can do is pray
He's tame and he talks
Though I must confess
I never did teach him
His name and address

Sarah Branfield

God's Gift

Some months ago my Bessie died.
With empty arms I cried and cried.

In a shop window on display
A notice with the words to say,
'A puppy needing someone who
Would care for her and love her too'.
Huddled there all alone,
I cuddled her, we then went home.
With TLC she's growing strong,
All her sadness now has gone.

Jenny's eyes look up to say
'So glad you came for me that day'.
With licks, cuddles, lots of fun,
Sure God sent this little one.
She's filled my empty heart and now,
She is my faithful loving pal.

Vera Hilton

My Blackbird

At the break of dawn he struts,
Like a proud peacock
On a power line,
Icicles glinting on his black feathers
Which are crystals
Glimmering in the cold morning light,
He seems unpeturbed by this
As he flies from rooftop to rooftop
Screaming at the other birds who dare defy him,
They gather on the roofs in lines,
As if waiting in a roll-call,
Standing as still and as lifeless as statues,
Not a movement is to be had from them,
But then at the flick of an eye they are gone
Flying away
To a world unknown
And untouched by the hand of man -
Only he stays, my blackbird.

Nishani Balendra

Tammy

She is an amber-eyed, long-haired, black,
fluffy-tailed, Persian cat.
(Not too thin, not too fat!)
Her owners divorced and gave all their animals away
so, this little darling was given to me - one day -

The moment I saw her 'it was love at first sight';
she was cowering down, shivering and full of fright,
therefore with reassuring words, I kept saying:
'Come on little one, everything will be alright!'

At first my attentions did not mean a lot,
until onto my lap she decided to hop,
'padding' with paws, continuously purring
and I comforted 'Tammy', offering plenty of nurturing.
Fascinating creatures with personalities so sweet,
clean, easy, curling up tight - to sleep -
after carefully selecting a particular seat . . .

A few years have passed and Tammy loves her domain;
over other 'moggies' she seems to reign!
I am not sure of her age, but she is quite wise
and when I return home from work, what a pleasant surprise,
my beautiful pet waiting for me - all alone -
near the gate, perched on a rather large stone.

D A Spence-Crawford

It's A Cat's Life

I often sit and watch my cat
And think I'd like a life like that
Meals on tap and treats galore
Love and attention, without lifting a paw
Toys for play, a warm bed for sleep
A lap, a cuddle and my heart to keep
No daily grind to earn a wage
Just the life of Riley, at any age
No worries or cares, free from strife
You're a lottery winner, when it's 'my' cat's life!

Lynn Greene

Mac

A little 'Aberdeen' we had
As friend throughout the War.
He was just the personality
That we were looking for.

Once, when our car, with open door,
Was ready parked outside,
He asked his Pekinese friend in,
To join him for a ride!

He loved games in the garden,
Chasing his ball (bright red),
But stopped it with his nose before
It trespassed on the bed.

He really didn't seem to mind
The 'flying bombs' at all,
Though when they fell, with deafening crash,
He scuttled down the hall!

This lion-hearted dog deserved
A shelter to himself.
He made his choice - our trolley -
And just curled up on the shelf!

E D Abbott

Slimbridge Sparrows

At end of trail they sit and wait
Amongst the willow leaves
A strong round pole, it acts as perch
From which they fly to feed.

The visitors they walk the paths
Past duck and geese in plenty
A bag of food to spread about
And each bird gains an entry.
Just a morsel so it's shared with
Everyone who asks - until you
Come to the winding lane, from
Where you will depart. The road
That is the last and
Here the sparrows sit and wait
As they've all thought without a doubt
You'll empty all remaining food
From bags, from hands you'll part
With all the seeds that's left
And where it's spilled deep in your coat
You'll turn your pockets inside out!

Joan Richardson

Tom Tom

We had a beautiful cat
Tom, Tom was his name
He sat so proud upon the fence
Surveying his domain.

He decided to move in with us
Many years ago
Although we would often cuss
Everybody loved him so.

His eyes were clear as crystal
Two jewels, of emerald green
His ginger coat, was soft as down
Always impeccably clean.

He would hunt amongst the gardens
Never showing any fear
No animal, or bird was safe
When his presence was so near.

After years of many battles
He grew weary, tired and weak
His lust for life, slowly drained
Till one day, he was laid to sleep.

An emptiness surrounds the house
We see things he loved to touch
All that's left are memories
Of ginger Tom, we loved so much . . .

GIG

The Swan

Gracefully flapping its wings
within confined space
of the shallow pond;
it dipped
its long neck
into the icy mirror.

At a glance it saw
its reflection,
humbly swam away
to the other side
floating on water,
like a galleon.

It bowed again
in a sign of prayer.

Raymond Fenech

The Little Fish

The fish that floats along the stream
its fins coloured by a silvery gleam
it mingles with the flowing splashes
unaware whereto it dashes

It is too minute to have the force
to turn and take another course
it is a captive of the torrent
though it finds it quite abhorrent

Whenever it tries to move aside
it is hurled back and has to slide
along the route outlined at start
being unable to depart

The little fish finds no way out
it doesn't know to pout or shout
it only hopes that in the end
it will not finish up in sand . . .

Wila Yagel

Our Sam

Samuel Ryan was just a cat, he wasn't bred for show
A tabby cat with attitude who knew what felines know
He came as just a kitten, too small to leave his mum
Nursed and loved through kittenhood Sam's life began its run

Our Sam was independent, he didn't give a damn
He made the world his oyster and make it work for Sam
He ate when he was hungry, he went just where he pleased
He tore up carpets on the stairs and shredded trunks of trees

He didn't have a love life, he got an early chop
But the life he had was kingly. our Samuel had the lot
The household moved around him, they nurtured every whim
Sam the Man ran the plan the house belonged to him

He sometimes let you stroke him to feel his soft smooth fur
And rarely did he deign to give a condescending purr
But Samuel in his old age became a loving friend
And rested quietly round the house in peace until the end.

Ray Ryan

Caught In The Act!

You'd never think he'd been fed today,
both breakfast and dinner
and treats as a winner
for being a good boy, okay.
See - he's got to the kitchen bin once more,
big nose in deep,
teeth gripping to keep
a hold on that scrap in his jaw.

No, Monty, *No!* You *can't* have that tin
of leftover beans -
You *know* what that means:
we'll both stay awake; you *shan't* win!
You'd never believe he's been so well fed
as with lid round his neck
and the kitchen a wreck,
I've just brushed more crumbs from his head!

He indeed was so lovingly looked after,
but altho' he was 'bold'
he got blind, ill and old,
and could no longer give me such laughter:
In '99 on 10th of November
he had his 'Big Sleep' -
now those images I keep
to cherish, to smile - and remember.

Ann Voaden

Jessie

She is a very beacon in the fog
The black and white contrasting, neatly drawn,
The tail's plume proudly like a pennant borne,
She is more like an angel than a dog!
Her joyful barks with little jumps agog,
With Jessie to the vibrant woods we're drawn,
Through springtime song, all bright the flowering thorn.
Now wakes the squirrel and the shy hedgehog,
Then gently, sweet, resting between her paws
Her head, with lovely eyes, so trusting, kind.
So sweet! She shares your bed and sings a song
Within this house she rules with friendly laws
No mean or common thought invades her mind
For she is faithful, brave and nobly strong!

H Hick

Our Friend Casey

Her mouth was solemn, her eyes were sad
Maybe, thinking of the sad life she had
But, out of the shadows, and into a dream
Rescued at last, her eyes lit a brief gleam

Out of Battersea's Dogs' Home, then to be free
Away from the protected shelter, to liberty
Happy, but strange, she must have felt, oft
Her head on one side, and her paws held aloft

Watching the fire, so warm with a glow
Feeling at home, how her eyes lit up so
Her form claimed the fireside, oh, what a treat
Knowing then, she was at home, far away from the retreat

While, taking her for walks, around the forest
With her leash off, to run like a greyhound, to show her best
Casey couldn't get home quick enough for her treats
Waiting, patiently, for her chews and biscuits

Never a threat, or a slap for any disaster
As, Casey was trained properly, by her new owner
Although she was perhaps, a few years old
When she was taken in, out from the cold

To punish herself, when she knew she was naughty
Taking herself into a room, and sending herself to Coventry
To sulk or sleep the whole night through
No sound came from her, till morn was in view.

So intelligent, gentle, and obedient, in her way
Since Casey our Dobermann, was claimed from those sad days
She was loved and cared for, right to the end
She was more than a pet, she was more than a friend.

Jean McGovern

A Tribute To Bess (Jelly Belly)

It all started fourteen years ago . . .

A little bundle round and fat,
that's how we first recall,
our memories of *Bess,*
the bestest dog of all.

She grew into a lovely lass,
sleek and proud,
a touch of class.
Loving, faithful, ever true,
A cherished Staffie,
That was *you.*

As the happy years quickly passed
you gave us memories to last,
and soon you looked as you had before,
round and fat,
sitting by the door,
waiting for your daily walk,
sometimes we felt, that you could talk.

A trusting friend,
Now gone to rest.
To us you were,
Simply the best!

J C Davies

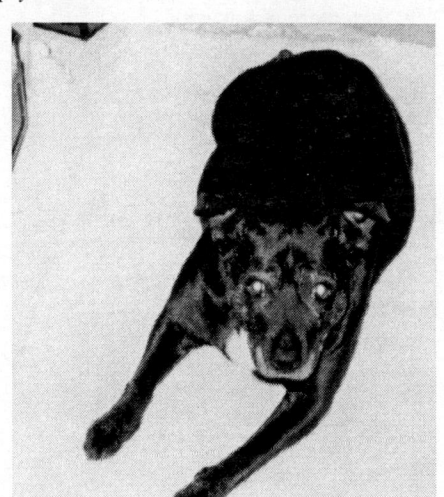

Gemma

(On the death of her mistress)

They told me that my mistress
Would not be gone too long,
But I waited and I waited,
And still she didn't come.

She didn't look too happy
As they helped her down the stairs,
They said that they would visit her,
Remember her in their prayers.

For several days they came and went
In hurry and in haste,
My longing looks and wagging tail
For 'walkies' seemed a waste.

Then came the day when muffled bells
Rang out from down the hill.
With tears they said goodbye to her -
She'll never more be ill.

For she has gone to heaven now,
It's made me very sad,
But I have got a family,
A brother, sister, dad:

And then there is a special friend
With whom I like to play.
We chase the bunnies up the lane,
When called - we run away!

I like to think my mistress
Would only be too glad
To know that though I miss her,
I am not *quite* so sad.

Jean Rees

Our Dog Prince

My brother gave you to us when you were a little pup.
We brought you home and gave you love
and spoiled you such a lot.

You fitted in so very nice, you were our pride and joy.
You were so very gentle with our two little boys.
You jumped around and played all day,
you gave the boys such pleasure.

When they went to school you would sit and cry
and look in wonder, oh why, oh why did they
not take me, I wouldn't be any bother.

I don't know how you knew it, but you always
seemed to know the time the boys came from school.
You'd sit by the door in silence waiting for
their sound and jump on them as they came
through the door.

You lived with us for fourteen years,
no trouble did you cause us.
We all loved you very much.
We didn't want to lose you.

But you were in so much pain we had to let you go.
You were such a faithful dog we couldn't
see you suffer.

So goodbye old friend of ours,
you are in our hearts forever.

R Danks

Kim

One day I went to market, just to browse around,
There I saw a farmer with a trailer as he drove into town.
Gazing through a net were some gorgeous little eyes,
They looked at me so pitiful, nearly made me cry.
I went a little closer to have a better look
When suddenly a man appeared, to write them down in his book.
With a number stuck upon them, as they were sold in lots.
I asked if I could buy one, the answer was 'Fraid not
You will have to bid for one, when I hold them up for sale.'
I walked away so sad, as they sat and wagged their tails.
To and fro I went to see, just what was going on,
The pup held up for sale, no bid came from anyone.
The auctioneer then looked around, what next should he do,
Officials walking up and down getting in a stew.
I myself got so worked up, no way could I keep calm,
When suddenly that pup I loved found comfort in my arms.
For fourteen years he was my friend I could not have wished for more
When I was ill he laid his head upon my knee, or watched me from the floor.
Then came the time, a grand old age, when he could no longer see
The sad day came when he fell asleep, God had called Kim home from me.

Mary Cousins

Meeting Brian

Under fifteen inches and nearly two feet long -
Whatever sort of dog is that? He really looks quite wrong.
I've met lots of other dachshunds, but they don't look the same.
And really, for a dachshund, he has got a funny name.
At first I thought he must be old, because of all that grey
Amongst the brindle colour, but you say he's made that way.
So he's a wire-haired dachshund, I've not seen one before.
His tongue must get quite dirty as it drags along the floor!

I've often watched you on your walks with Brian running free,
Or standing with one paw in air, or playing round a tree.
I've rarely seen a dog with such emotion in his face.
Sometimes laughing, sometimes frowning or doleful in disgrace.
He's such a lively character, to whom each day's such fun.
I can't believe you're ever cross, whatever he has done!

Good heavens, what a mournful howl, like baying at the moon.
He doesn't like car sirens or an ice-cream van's high tune!
I really can't help laughing, who would have thought that note
Could emanate with such a force from such a little throat!

You say you take him everywhere, on foot or in the car,
What about your holidays, I suppose you can't go far?
As long as he is with you, he doesn't mind the longest trip.
You've been this year to Scotland, and even Ireland on a ship.
Well Brian, what a clever boy you are, to sail upon the sea.
I've never been upon a boat, you're more venturesome than me.
You're getting him a passport, so you can go abroad?
It's clear to me this little dog won't ever be lonely or bored.

Oh dear, I think perhaps that we have talked a bit too long.
Was that a whining sound I heard, ah now a great big yawn.
Just one last pat before you leave, now off you go and play.
I'll look for you tomorrow, for you've really made my day.

Lucy M Kaye

Old Shep

My darling wee Shep I miss you so much
You have gone from this life
But left me your love
Which I will cherish forever
As once you did too
For you gave me a love
Which was faithful and true.

M E Smith

The Stray

We didn't choose him, he chose us
A ginger, furry, loving puss.
The night was wet and dark,
The dog next door was heard to bark
When suddenly above it rose
A yowling and a tapping close
To home. We looked to see
What shook the door so urgently,
And stretched on hind legs beating paws
With mouth wide open, teeth and claws
All to tell of desperate need
A cat in want of warmth indeed.
'Oh go away, and find your home
You naughty cat so far to roam.'
'I have no home' he seemed to say,
'Oh let me stay - one night - one day.'
The door we opened, just a crack
And after that - no going back.
His wet form sprang on each one's knee
'Oh look how loving I can be
Just hear my purr and feel me throb
I'm not a cat who'd ever rob,
But I will rid your home of mice
On little food will I suffice.'
We kept the cat, and sure he brought
A thieving mouse that he had caught.
What's more he brought deep love to us
That wild and homeless ginger puss.

Hazel Browne

Smoky

You turned up from nowhere
sent to me because I care
I love you so for you are part
of me now, but you break my heart
when you don't eat and run away
stay out at night until next day
I know you're ill, the vet had said
fish I buy so you will be fed
not much else that you will eat
so cook it for you, a daily treat.
I brushed your fur until it shone
now the lustre and shine has gone.
You sit upon the back of my chair
and tug away at my hair.
You used to play and have fun
now it takes all your time to run
at a slower pace than before
not up to old tricks anymore
jumping on your sister and brother
but instead you come to Mother.
You lift up your head for a kiss
my poor darling how I shall miss
the little cry when you want attention
and all things that we won't mention
not long now before you're in heaven
my darling boy, you are only just seven.

Eunice Neale

Skippy Mulldoon

Skippy Mulldoon is a Bichion
All white with a black button nose
He skips round the house with a frolic
Never cares about wanting to pose
He sleeps in his house without stirring
At the side or the foot of the bed
Sometimes he's so wicked he wares me
And leaves me shaking my head
But Skip is a great little fellow
With a welcome so warm and so great
He gives you a feeling of love
A feeling of never wanting to hate.

Glenys M Bowell

One Man And His Dog, Simba

(On arriving back from washing up at the Wishing Well café)

Woof woof
Wag wag
Hello Tim . . .
Nice to see you again
(I have to say I've been missing him) . . .

You're back from the Wishing Well . . .
Where all that tasty food's been cooked
All the scents I can smell . . .
There's cabbage, potatoes and lamb . . .
Chocolate cake
And oh sniff, sniff . . . ham . . .

There's dry milk and coffee on your arm
There's a scent of perfume . . .
Did the girls warm to your charm?

Hello Sim
Thanks for welcoming me home
You're a great fellow
Here's your bone . . .

T A Saunders

It's Only A Dog

It's only a dog with a leg at each corner,
It will fit in somewhere, it's only a stray,
And that was the last word I had to say.
It's only a dog with a leg at each corner,
Soft turned-down ears with long pointed nose
Bright brown eyes and very large teeth.

It's only a dog with a leg at each corner,
We'll give it a box in the kitchen,
But it lies on the sofa and watches TV
It's only a dog with a leg at each corner,
It sleeps in the bedroom, on the bed, when I'm gone,
Only a dog with a leg at each corner
Until the day he died,
Then I cried.

Peter E Smith

Truffles

I once had a rabbit called Truffles.
Biscuity coloured, all fluffles.
A cuddly bun and a treasure,
Who daily his hutch he would measure.
No problems, hang-ups or snuffles.

But he never went *out* to lunch.
He liked the *in*side of his hutch
Though he'd the full right to roam,
In sun or rain he'd stay home
And enjoy his lingering munch.

I *could* plonk him down on the grass.
He'd hop all around and there pass
The plants you'd thought bunnies love
Then return to 'Chez nous' up above.
Did you ever hear such a farce?

One day, my own mum, she died.
And oh, how I cried and I cried.
But my long-term sadness departed!
A new phase of life had now started!
My family bonds were untied.

In a very short time after,
Imagine my joy and my laughter,
When my rabbit at home
Was now seen to roam
And never returned to his quarters!

A change then, in both me and bun,
We both found a garden of fun!
Truffles, once all lethargic
Changed almost like magic
And stayed all day out in the sun.

But even while I watched, ecstatic,
The fox watch caused an act drastic.
Though I could not catch him,
My bun met his match and
That was the end - very tragic!

The old empty hutch is now weathered.
I remain living, untethered!
Parallels I'll not draw,
Though struck to the core
When Truffles' sweet life, it was severed.

Depressions's a sad mental tumour,
I know this is true, not a rumour,
Though his memory fades,
I loved God's visual aid,
Sure He has a great sense of humour!

Laila Lacey

My Dog Bonnie

Did you ever see my dog, Bonnie? She was a dog with a heart of gold,
She came to me one December, as a puppy, just six weeks old,
She was brought in a wicker basket, with a blanket to keep her warm,
Then out she scampered and nipped me, and that's how our bond was formed.

She was as black as midnight can be, but her toes were tipped with white,
On her breast was a small white ripple, and her eyes were clear and bright,
She was Bonnie by name and nature, and came from a champion's line,
A Staffordshire bitch bull-terrier, I was proud to call her mine.

She loved to see all children, for as we passed the long school rail,
A score of hands would touch her, and Bonnie would lick them and wag her tail,
She could jump and run like a whirlwind, to snatch a ball from the air,
Then bring it back and taunt me, to take it, if I dare.

For twelve long years I walked her, every day, for many a mile,
Then we'd doze in the old grey armchair and Bonnie would dream awhile,
For her body would twitch and tremble as she played a phantom game,
And her legs would keep on running, till I softly called her name.

For twelve long years I loved her, and I know she loved me too,
But again the month was December, when I learned Bonnie's life was through.
As she lay in my arms that morning, and passed to eternal sleep,
Raindrops spattered the window, as the heavens began to weep.

And I'm not ashamed to tell you, that as I kissed my Bonnie goodbye,
Teardrops scalded my eyelids, for how could I keep them dry?
It's eight years now since I lost her, but in memory she's with me still,
For I feel her presence around me, and I know I always will.

Ralph Davis

Gizmo

I came to them a fluffy ball,
They knew I wouldn't grow very tall.
They gave me lots and lots of cuddles,
I gave them lots of puddles.
I chewed the hearth and scratched the door,
Until they could take no more.
I then decided to mend my ways
To be a creep certainly pays.
Sit on their knee, give them a lick,
It really is a very good trick.
I've got a thing about pants, bras and socks,
I hide them away in my toy box.
Paper hankies I love to eat,
Much more tasty than a bowl of meat.
Run round the house, jump on the bed,
Stop that Gizzy, my mum said.
Dad likes a play and a fight,
If I win then that's alright.
Bury a bone, but not very well,
They know where it's hid, I can tell.
Mum thinks her friend comes for a chat and some tea
But really she comes to visit me.
She thinks I am such a good boy,
I sit on her knee, then fetch a toy.
Peace and quiet sit with a chew,
There's only so much a dog can do.
Snuggled up in my quilt with my ted,
It's now time to go to bed.
Tomorrow I think that I will be good,
Just like a little Chihuahua should.

Elaine Taylor

Poor Innocence

I'd like to tell you a story, one that's sad but true
About a poor young horse and all that he went through.

He used to be a racehorse, silky, sleek and fast
Beating all the others as the winning post flew past.

He was a glowing chestnut with shining mane and tail
And in everything he entered, he would rarely fail.

Then one day when out riding he suddenly went lame
And from that day forward, he could never be raced again.

So he went to a new owner who took him far away
And dumped him on some scrubland with a solitary bale of hay.

Soon enough the hay ran out, leaving only weeds
And his owner never came to give him any feeds.

Very slowly time went past with the racehorse losing peak
Till there was no fodder left and he lay down feeling weak.

Then before he knew it, winter had closed in
Still he survived on nothing while his owner felt no sin.

It was freezing cold and he was covered in mud
He was as thin as a rake and coughing up blood.

In about midwinter he was laid out on the floor
Praying God would take him, for he cared no more.

When next he struggled to his feet, much to his surprise
He found himself in a stable with food before his eyes.

He gradually awoke himself and once or twice he shook
Then towards his feedbowl a shaky step he took.

When he finished eating he felt quite warm inside
For the fact that someone saved him, from where he would have died.

How do I know about this horse? Well, it's plain to see
I felt everything he went through, for that horse was me!

So listen very carefully to these words I say
If you have an animal, treasure him every day.

Dawn Gillam

Absolute Animals

Information

We hope you have enjoyed reading this book - and that you will continue to enjoy it in the coming years.

If you like reading and writing poetry drop us a line, or give us a call, and we'll send you a free information pack.

Write To

Triumph House Information
Remus House
Coltsfoot Drive
Woodston
Peterborough
PE2 9JX
(01733) 898102